MOSCOW

THE KREMLIN. RED SQUARE. ALL MOSCOW. TRINITY–ST SERGIUS MONASTERY

P-2 • 2003 • AMARANT

Text by T. Geidor and I. Kharitonova
Design by N. Kutovoy. Translated from the Russian by J. Redkina
Photography by A. Aleksandrov, Yu. Artamonov, R. Beniaminson, P. Demidov, Yu. and O. Grigorov, V. Khmelevsky,
V. Korniushin, V. Melnikov, V. Mendeleyev, V. Poliakov, N. Rakhmanov, V. Savik, A. Shabanov, V. Solomatin,
E. Steinert, O. Trubsky, V. Vdovin, A. Viktorov and A. Zakharchenko. Edited by I. Lvova. Colour correction
by L. Kornilova and S. Ludzsky. Published in association with A. Kudriavtsev and A. Kuznetsov

The Kremlin. Red Square

For centuries Moscow has been a treasure house of carefully preserved national cultural tradition. All the Russian tsars and emperors were crowned here in Russia's main cathedral, the ancient Dormition Cathedral, and both Peter the Great and Catherine the Great came to Moscow to celebrate their military victories. In 1812 the city was a sacrifice on the altar of war, yet precipitated the inglorious demise of Napoleon's great army. In May 1945 it greeted the victorious Russian troops coming back from Germany.

The Kremlin is Moscow's central architectural ensemble, the heart of Russia and symbol of her greatness. It is situated on the high bank of the Moscow River, at the mouth of the Neglinnaya (put into a conduit in the course of sanitation work and the city centre reconstruction, in 1816–20). This is the oldest part of Moscow, that as far back as the 11th century was the site of the Slaviansky town and its first manuscript reference dates from 1147.

In the reign of Yury Dolgoruky it was surrounded by a moat with ramparts. In the early 14th century Moscow became capital of the principality with the white-stone Kremlin developing into an impregnable fortress.

Towards the end of the 15th century, when the Moscow principality was transformed into the state of Muscovy, the Kremlin assumed a new significance, it was rebuilt and enlarged. It was then that the ensemble's style was mainly formed, its area of 27.5 hectares being enclosed with new mighty fortified structures. Majestic new cathedrals replaced the former white-stone churches on Sobornaya and Ivanovskaya Squares, which now seemed too small, and the princes' and boyars' dwellings stretched from the slope of Borovitsky Hill to the western section of the fortified wall. This notable period of construction work was carried out by Italian architects invited to Russia by Ivan III. They included Aristotele Fioravanti, Alovisio di Carcanno, Marco Ruffo, Pietro Solario and Antonio Gilardi. The Italian masters succeeded in creating essentially Russian forms of church architecture that served as models for subsequent construction over the following two centuries.

Further development of the Kremlin as an ideological, political and cultural centre was impelled by the growth and territorial expansion of the capital. Intensive building in the 17th century transformed the Kremilin, giving it the characteristics we see today. The Terem Palace and its churches, the Poteshny (Amusement) Palace (site of the first theatrical performances in Russia) and the Patriarch Courtyard with the Cathedral of the Twelve Apostles were erected, and the towers were topped with many-tiered hipped roofs. In the 18th and 19th centuries major construction and reconstruction work was carried out in the palace complex and the state administration buildings: the Arsenal, Great Kremlin Palace, Senate and Armoury all date from the period. The best Russian architects participated in it – Bartolommeo Rastrelli, Nikolay Lvov, Vasily Bazhenov, Matvey Kazakov, Konstantin Thon and Carlo Rossi.

In the Soviet epoch the Monastery of the Miracle (Chudov) and the Ascension Monastery were demolished along with a great number of churches. The Palace of Congresses was built next to the Patriarch Palace between 1959 and 1961.

The fortified structures of the Moscow Kremlin are best examples of mediaeval European fortifications. They were erected between 1485 and 1495 by the Italian architects Marco Ruffo, Antonio Gilardi, Pietro Antonio and Alovisio Antonio Solario. The vast territory of the Kremlin situated on lofty Borovitsky Hill at the confluence of two navigable rivers, the Moscow and the Neglinnaya, has the shape of an irregular triangle. The fortress walls have an overall length of 2 235 m. Along the perimeter stand eighteen fortified towers, with the Kutafya Tower overlooking the Troitsky Bridge across the River Neglinnaya. Faced with large, well-baked

View of Red Square from the Spasskaya Tower

bricks weighing 8 kg each, the walls are from 5 to 19 m high depending on the reilef detail, and from 3.5 to 6.5 m thick as far as the merlons. Multi-tiered towers, originally crowned with flat platforms for accurate aim in the traditional manner of European fortresses, were elevated with the addition of tall hipped roofs in the 17th century. They reach a height of 28 to 71 m, the Spasskaya (Saviour) and Troitskaya (Trinity) being the tallest.

View of Kremlin's walls and towers

Taynitskaya Tower. 1485.
Architect Antonio Friazin and others

Konstantino-Yeleninskaya, Nabatnaya and Spasskaya Towers. 1490s. Architect Pietro Antonio Solario.
Hipped roofs added in the 17th century

Troitskaya Tower. 1495
Kutafya Tower. 1516. Architect Antonio Friazin

Spasskaya Tower. 1491. Architect Pietro Antonio Solario;
1624–25. Architect Bazhen Ogurtsov. Clockwork design by
Christofer Halloway

CATHEDRAL OF THE DORMITION

The Cathedral of the Dormition used to be Russia's main cathedral. It was built in 1475–79 on the site of the original white-stone church by order of Ivan III, Grand Prince of Muscovy. Though the cathedral was designed by the Italian architect and engineer Aristotele Fioravanti, its style and composition is consistent with the strict rules of the Orthodox canon. Fragments of the original frescoes painted by a team of artists working under the guidance of the famous Russian icon-painter Dionysius have been preserved in the sanctuary (chancel). Other frescoes were executed in the 17th century by masters from various Russian towns, led by court icon-painters Ivan and Boris Paisein. The south, north and west walls are lined with the tombs of metropolitans and patriarchs. The heads of the Russian Orthodox Church had been buried here until 1721,

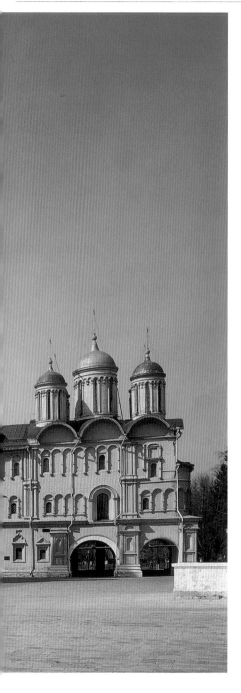

*Cathedral of the Dormition. 1475–79.
Architect Aristotele Fioravanti*

Cathedral of the Dormition. Interior

The Fiery Eye of the Saviour *icon.
1340s. From the* Local Saints *tier in the
iconostasis of the Cathedral
of the Dormition*

Fresco on the altar screen. Cathedral of the Dormition. 1481

when Peter the Great abolished the patriarchate and introduced administration by the Synod. The remains of the first metropolitan of Moscow lie in the north sanctuary. Metropolitan Peter founded the metropolitan cathedra (chair) in the new Russian capital and initiated construction of the first white-stone Cathedral of the Dormition in 1326. An icon preserved in the cathedral portrays Metropolitan Peter in the centre and episodes from his life in borderscenes, including erection of the cathedral. The most important state ceremonies were held in the Cathedral of the Dormition: ordination of metropolitans and patriarchs, coronation of tsars and later emperors and public proclamation of state edicts. During its existence the cathedral was decorated with the finest examples of ancient Russian art, in particular icons from the 12th to 17th centuries.

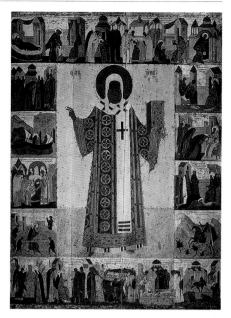

Works of art collected by the grand princes, tsars, metropolitans and patriarchs formed the basis of the state treasury: priceless manuscripts and art objects fashioned from gold and silver and decorated with precious stones, that were crafted by the best painters, jewellers, engravers, metalworkers, embroiderers and gilders. After the closure of the cathedral in 1919 most of the collection was transferred to the Armoury, and many icons to the Tretyakov Gallery.

Icon of Metropolitan Peter with scenes from his life. By Dionysius (?). Late 15th to early 16th century

Royal place of Ivan the Terrible. 1551

Cathedral of the Annunciation. 1485–89; 1562–64

The Transfiguration *icon. By Andrey Rublev. 1405. From the* Feasts *tier in the iconostasis of the Cathedral of the Annunciation*

CATHEDRAL OF THE ANNUNCIATION

The Cathedral of the Annunciation was built in 1485–89 as the domestic church of the tsars and grand princes of Muscovy. It was included in the complex of royal residences and palace buildings. The cathedral stands on the basement of an ancient 14th-century church. It was here that the tsar and his family celebrated christenings, weddings and daily prayers.

The interior is richly decorated. The many-tiered gilded iconostasis features a number of icons painted by Andrey Rublev and Theophanes the Greek, the renowned master icon-painters of the late 14th and early 15th centuries. The cathedral also contains frescoes painted in 1508 by a team of court painters headed by Theodosius, son of the famous Dionysius. After the fire in 1547 Novgorod and Pskov masters repainted the damaged frescoes. The vivid, intense colourscale matches that of the luxurious royal chambers linked to the cathedral by special passageways. The floor is inlaid with tiles of agate jasper. The sumptuousness of the royal cathedral is embellished by cast iron doors.

Cathedral of the Annunciation. Iconostasis

◀ *Cupolas of the Terem churches.*
1684. Architect Osip Startsev

Church of the Deposition of the Robe.
1484–86

Cathedral of the Archangel Michael.
1505–08. Architect Alovisio Novo

CHURCH OF THE DEPOSITION OF THE ROBE

The domestic church of Russian metropolitans and patriarchs stands by the west portal of the Annunciation Cathedral. It was built by Pskov architects between 1484 and 1486 in the style of early Moscow architecture. Rebuilding in the 16th to 18th centuries resulted in a number of alterations, but restoration work conducted from the 1930s to 1960s has reinstated the church's original appearance.

The frescoes preserved inside the church were painted by court masters Ivan Borisov, Sidor Pospeyev, Semion Avraamov in 1643–44. The icons are of an earlier date, completed by the patriarchal icon-painter Nazary Istomin in 1627. The Church of the Deposition of the Robe became part of the royal palace complex after construction of the new patriarchal Church of the Twelve Apostles in the mid-17th century.

A collection of Russian woodcarving from the 16th to 18th centuries is also preserved here.

CATHEDRAL OF THE ARCHANGEL MICHAEL

The cathedral which served as the burial place of the grand princes and tsars of Muscovy stands on the site of an ancient church built in the early 14th century and dedicated to the Archangel Michael, a guardian angel of the Moscow princes in war time. The present-day cathedral was erected between 1505 and 1508 by the Venetian architect Alovisio Novo and painted by the best masters from Moscow, Yaroslavl and Kostroma: Yakov Kazanets, Stepan Rezanets, Simon Ushakov, Iosif Vladimirov, Gury Nikitin, Fyodor Zubov and others. All the grand princes and tsars prior to Peter the Great are buried in the cathedral. A carved white-stone canopy by the south-east pillar covers the grave of the murdered Tsarevich Dmitry, sanctified as a holy martyr.

Icon of the Archangel Michael. First third of the 15th century.
From the Local Saints *tier in the iconostasis of the Cathedral*
of the Archangel Michael

Cathedral of the Archangel Michael. Iconostasis

Patriarch Palace and the Church of the Twelve Apostles. 1642–55. Architects David Okhlebinin, Antip Konstantinov and Averky Makeyev

In 1505–08 a bell tower some 60 m high was put up above the existing Church of St John Climacus which was accordingly named in honour of the saint: "Ivan (John) the Great". In 1600 the tower was extended to a height of 81 m. The Church with the Bell Tower of the Ressurection of Christ was added to the north flank between 1532 and 1534. It houses the largest bell in Russia still in working order — the Dormition, or Festive, Bell.

By the north facade of the Dormition Cathedral stands the Patriarch Courtyard complex. It was built under Patriarch Nikon who ordered extensive replacement and partial reconstruction of the older buildings in the mid-1650s. It was as spacious and luxurious as the Palace of the Tsar Alexey Mikhailovich. The new domestic church, the Church of the Twelve Apostles, was erected above the gateway leading to the Patriarch Courtyard.

The Faceted Palace is the oldest secular building in Moscow. It was part of the palace complex of grand princes and was used for ceremonial receptions. Built by order of Ivan III the palace owes its name to the decorative stonework on its eastern facade. The porch removed during the palace reconstruction in the 1930s was rebuilt in 1994. It used to play an important ceremonial role as the main entrance to the palace's throne room, processions passed through here at coronations, weddings and church festivals. The original frescoes that once decorated the Faceted Palace have been destroyed and replaced by those painted in 1883 by the Belousov brothers, master craftsmen from the village of Palekh, who used the technique of the famous icon-painter Simon Ushakov.

Kremlin bell towers. 1505–08. Architect Bon Friazin; 1532–43. Architect Petrok Maly; 1600, 1624. Architect Bazhen Ogurtsov

Sobornaya Square. The Faceted Palace. 1487–1591. Architects Marco Ruffo and Pietro Solario

Faceted Palace. Interior ▶

Grand Kremlin Palace. 1838–50. Architect Konstantin Thon

GRAND KREMLIN PALACE

Grand Kremlin Palace. State room

The magnificent building of the Kremlin Palace was constructed on the site of ancient palace structures. The vast square edifice consists of 700 rooms with an area of approximately 20 000 m².

Moscow architects N. Chichagov, F. Richter, N. Shokhin and P. Gerasimov took part in the construction using in their work mediaeval architectural tradition. They also designed the interiors.

Service areas and the private apartments of the imperial family were situated on the ground floor. All the interiors are noted for their sumptuous furnishing. State rooms on the second floor are named after Russian orders of St George, St Vladimir and St Catherine, and these were restored after the reconstruction of the 1930s. The largest and grandest room is that dedicated to the Order of St George, the patron saint of Russian warfare. This medal is awarded for bravery in battle.

Cupolas of the Kremlin cathedrals

Terem Palace. Golden Porch. Detail

*Terem Palace. One of the vaulted 17-th century rooms.
Murals painted by T. Kiselyov after the drawings by Fyodor Solntsev. 1836–38*

Terem Palace. 1635–36. Architects Antip Konstantinov, Bazhen Ogurtsov, Trefil Sharutin and Larion Ushakov

TEREM PALACE

It is included in the Grand Kremlin Palace complex. The Terem Palace with its state rooms of the tsar was once part of the ancient ensemble of palace buildings. It was put up on the two-tier basement dating from 1494. On the lower floor there were service areas and kitchens, and on the first floor articles of ceremonial attire were made in the Masterskaya (Workshop) Room. The second floor was occupied by offices and the quarters of the tsar's personal guards. The tsar's apartments took up the entire third floor of the palace while the upper floor, or Teremok, was a large vaulted children's room where the tsar's sons lived including the future Emperor Peter the Great. The original murals were the work of court painters under Simon Ushakov, famous for his original new methods of icon-painting. They no longer exist. The existing murals date from 1836.

State Armoury. 1844–51. Architect Konstantin Thon

Royal regalia, emblems of imperial power

*Sabre in sheath. 1829.
Master Ivan Bushuyev*

STATE ARMOURY

This is the oldest museum in Russia since the collection was started by the grand princes of Muscovy in the 14th and 15th centuries long before the Armoury Palace itself was established. The Treasure House, the first depository for valuables, was built in the Kremlin in 1485. The Armoury is first mentioned in a chronicle dating from 1547. Originally it was used not only as a treasure house for valuable art objects but also as a workshop where both ceremonial and martial arms were produced. In addition to the armourers there were engravers, metalworkers, bone-carvers, gilders and filigreeworkers. In the 18th century production ceased, and towards the beginning of the 19th century the Armoury received the status of royal museum. Nowadays this is one of the finest collections of Russian and foreign decorative and applied art from the 4th to early 20th centuries. One of the most valuable pieces is the famous Monomachus cap, the crown of Russian tsars. According to legend the Monomachus cap was sent to the Russian grand prince by Byzantine Emperor Constantine Monomachus. Since 1547 it has been used to crown the Russian tsars.

*Treasures from the State Armoury and the Diamond Fund
of Russia* ▶

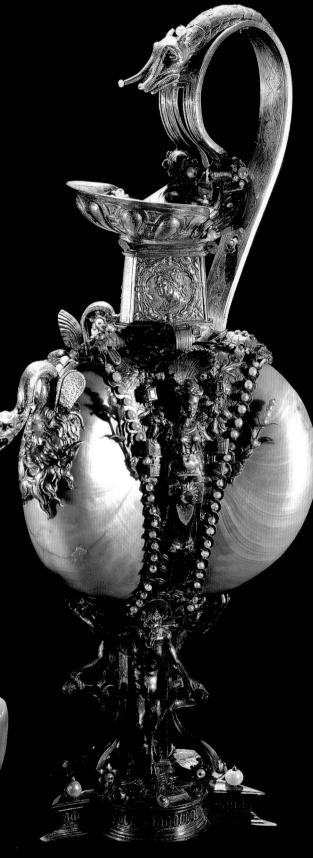

Throughout the history of Moscow Red Square has been integral part of the Kremlin ensemble. Its original name was Poloye ("waste") place, or Pozhar. Later it turned into the city's main market place known as Torg. In the 17th century it was given its present-day name of Red Square which means "beautiful" in Slavonic. The square has been the stage of most important events in Russian history. It witnessed long festive religious processions, royal trains and arrivals of foreign embassies. People crowded here to listen to the royal edicts that were proclaimed from Lobnoye Mesto ("place of a skull") — a circular platform faced with stone slabs. Lobnoye Mesto was also the site of public prayers and executions.

Tsar Cannon. 1586. Gunsmith Andrey Chokhov

*Tsar Bell. 1733–35.
Founders Ivan and Mikhail Motorin*

View of Red Square and the Cathedral of St Basil the Blessed

Monument to Kuzma Minin and Dmitry Pozharsky. 1804–18. Sculptor Ivan Martos

In 1612 the Russian army led by Kuzma Minin and Dmitry Pozharsky marched through Red Square to the Kremlin to drive the Poles out. To commemorate the event the monument to Minin and Pozharsky was set up here in 1818. In 1812 Napoleon inspected his troops on the square, yet soon suffered a crushing defeat. In 1945 after the end of World War II, the Victory Parade was held on Red Square, with soldiers from all the fronts taking part.

In its architectural perfection and beauty Red Square can rival the most famous squares in the world like Piazza di San Marco in Venice, square in front of St Peter's Cathedral in Rome and Place de la Concorde in Paris.

Cathedral of the Intercession. View from Vasilyevsky Spusk (descent)

CATHEDRAL OF THE INTERCESSION (CATHEDRAL OF ST BASIL THE BLESSED)

The cathedral has been a branch of the State Historical Museum since 1928. It was built by order of Ivan the Terrible and with the blessing of Metropolitan Macarius. The cathedral was to commemorate an important event — the victory of the Russian army over the Kazan Khanate and final liberation from the Tartar-Mongol yoke, as a result of which the Russian lands were united round Moscow as their capital. The concept of a cathedral–monument brought forth the unusual architectural forms: nine churches are set on a lofty pedestal, eight of them are grouped round the central Church of the Intercession, whose hipped roof towers above the others at a height of 47.5 m. In 1588 the popular "fool for Christ" Vasily, or Basil the Blessed, was buried in the north-east corner of the cathedral. A tenth church dedicated to St Basil was added to the existing structure directly above his tomb, and since then the whole ensemble is commonly referred to as the Cathedral of St Basil the Blessed.

Cathedral of the Intercession 'at-the-Moat' (Cathedral of St Basil the Blessed). 1555–61. Architects Barma and Postnik

All Moscow

The date of Moscow's foundation is lost in the remote past. Tradition says that in the 9th century Prince Oleg founded a town on the River Smorodinka (now the Moscow River). The fact is proved by some articles of daily use dating from the period which have been found in the excavations on the site.

A settlement might have existed here before 1147 — the year under which Moscow is for the first time mentioned in the chronicle as the place where Princes Sviatoslav of Chernigov and Yury of Suzdal (Dolgoruky) met in the course of internecine conflicts. According to tradition those lands were owned by a boyar Kuchka whom Prince Yury executed and founded a town on his former estate with the centre in Borovichi (the site of the present-day Kremlin). In the 15th century Moscow included several districts — the Kremlin, Posad, Zagorod and Zamoskvorechye; it was the recognized capital of Russian princes and leading trading town.

MANEGE AND THEATRE SQUARES

After the victory over Napoleon in 1812 and after the catastrophic retreat of the French troops Moscow was rapidly restored and rebuilt. In 1817 a new plan for the development of the ancient capital was introduced by the specially organized Construction Committee. It launched a great program of rebuilding, which included a partial replanning of the city centre. The Russian architect Osip Bove played a big part in its work. In accordance with the 1817 plan a number of famous architectural ensembles appeared in Moscow and some improvements were made in the area round the Kremlin. The system of water basins and canals dating from the 18th century, when the Neglinnaya River bed had been reconstructed, was filled in and the Neglinnaya was diverted into a subterranian conduit. In 1821–23 Bove laid out the Alexander Gardens near the Kremlin wall where the Grotto and the Gate were erected soon after. In 1822 the architect F. Shestakov designed and built the fence around the Gardens.

At that time Manege Square was being formed. In 1817 the monumental edifice of Manege designed by Bove and Spanish engineer A. Betancourt was erected in the square, its architectural form being simple,

yet imposing. The Manege's mighty Doric colonnade topped by the massive pediment without any sculptural decoration dominates the square. The unique wooden framework of its ceiling was considered a wonder of technology: the ceiling has a span of 45 m with no support in the middle. The Manege was intended for army drills and parades and its interior was so spacious that a whole regiment numbering about 2 000 soldiers could freely manoeuvre inside. Nowadays most representative Moscow, all-Russia and international shows are held here. Its exhibition area is 6 500 m².

In 1817–19 another Classical architect Domenico Gilliardi restored the building of Moscow University damaged in the war of 1812, which still stands in the square. Manege Square also features two largest hotels of the capital — the *National* built in the beginning of 20th century and *Moscow* erected on Manege Square only in 1933-35. This high-rise building now dominate the place.

In accordance with the new plan the Kitay-gorod territory was bounded with a semicircular chain of public squares starting up from the Moscow River and linked with the Kremlin esplanade by Theatre Square.

It was then that the square assumed its present-day rectangular shape with one side slanted by the Kitay-gorod wall. To rebalance the irregularity a triangular garden was laid out by the wall. Located on the opposite side in the middle is the Bolshoi (Petrovsky) Theatre. The edifice decorated with a monumental eight-column portico emphasizes the main axis of the square. Also on Theatre Square is the Maly (Little) Theatre.

National *hotel. 1903.*
Architect A. Ivanov

National *hotel. Detail of the facade*

Moscow *hotel. 1933–35. Architects*
A. Shchusev, L. Savelyev and
O. Stapran; 1968–77.
Architects A. Boretsky, D. Solopov
and I. Rozhin

Fountain in Manege Square. 1990s.
Sculptor Z. Tsereteli

Bolshoi Theatre. Auditorium

Bolshoi Theatre. 1821–24. Architects O. Bove and A. Mikhailov; 1855–56. Architect A. Kavos

BOLSHOI THEATRE. *METROPOL* HOTEL

The building of the Bolshoi Theatre is one of the best examples of Russian architecture from the mid-19th century and a largest theatre structure in Europe. It is the leading opera house of the country. Staged here have been operas by Mikhail Glinka, Modest Moussorgsky, Alexander Borodin, Nikolay Rimsky-Korsakov, operas and ballets by Pyotr Tchaikovsky. The theatre has been famous for its brilliant singers, dancers, conductors and stage-set artists. Such names as Fyodor Chaliapin, Leonid Sobinov, Antonina Nezhdanova, Yekaterina Geltser, Sergey Rakhmaninov and Konstantin Korovin are the pride of both Russian and world musical culture. The famous Russian singers Ivan Kozlovsky, Sergey Lemeshev, Nadezhda Obukhova, Maria Maksakova and ballet dancers Marina Semenova, Galina Ulanova, Asaf Messerer and Olga Lepeshinskaya performed here. Among the company's best productions are operas *Boris Godunov*, *Khovanshchina*, *Sadko*, *War and Peace*, *Othello*, *Aida*, *Don Carlos* and ballets *The Fountain of Bakhchisarai*, *Swan Lake*, *Nutcracker*, *Romeo and Juliet*, *Spartak* and many others.

The *Metropol* hotel designed in the early 20th century in the Art Nouveau style is also to be found in Theatre Square. Its plain facades are rather impressive. The ground floor is made of red granite and the upper floors are crowned with a big sculptured frieze and a ceramic panel *Princess Reverie* by Mikhail Vrubel. The sophisticated silhouette of the top part forms the smooth line of the roof against the blue sky.

Metropol hotel. 1899–1903. Architect V. Walcott ▶

State Pushkin Museum of Fine Arts. 1898–1912. Architect R. Klein, sculptor G. Zaleman

STATE PUSHKIN MUSEUM OF FINE ARTS

The world-famous Museum of Fine Arts is a major centre for the study of Western European art in Russia, second only in importance and scope to the renowned Hermitage in St Petersburg. The idea of creating a collection within the fine art and antiquities department of Moscow University which would cover all periods in the development of world art history and above all act as an educational institution received public approval in the mid-19th century. Philologist, art historian and Moscow University professor Ivan Tsvetayev was charged with formulating the aims of the project, devising a programme and organizing all planning and building work. Later he became the first museum curator.

The new museum was financed by leading Moscow patrons of arts: noblemen, industrialists and merchants. Many of them sat on the Founding Committee, whose president was a representative of the imperial family, Grand Duke Sergey Alexandrovich. Donations were received from A. Armand, N. Bogolepov, S. Mamontov, A. Mein, S. Morozov, A. and N. Shcherbatov, D. Khomyakov, Z. and F. Yusupov and others. The major industrialist and former student of Moscow University Yu. Nechayev-Maltsev made a particular important contribution.

In 1896 the City Duma granted a plot of land in the centre of Moscow to assist the University in carrying out their noble aim. In the same year a competition was announced for the best architectural composition. The gold medal was won by the Moscow architect Roman Klein, and construction lasted from 1898 to 1912.

The building assumed the form of a Greek temple on a high podium, with a Ionic colonnade at the central facade. The first-floor rooms have glass ceilings designed by the well-known engineers I. Rerberg and V. Shukhov. Expertise gained from the museums at Dresden and Berlin was used to create the new Moscow

Main staircase of the museum

museum. Russian and foreign scholars were consulted to establish the purposes and programmes of the museum.

The Alexander III Museum of Fine Arts affiliated to Moscow University was opened on May 31, 1912. A major part were plaster or metal casts and copies of mosaics or murals taken directly from the originals in workshops abroad. The unique collection of 6 000 ancient Egyptian artifacts made by famous scholar and egyptologist V. Golenishchev was a most valuable part of the museum holdings. In 1910 the museum was given some ninety 13th – 15th century Italian art works, one of the first collections to be donated. The museum became independent of the University in 1923.

In the 1920s and 1930s the holdings increased considerably after nationalization of private art collections, reorganization of the Moscow Public and Rumyantsev Museums, the addition of collections from the country estates outside Moscow and the closure of the Ostroukhov Museum of Painting and Icon-painting. Later, in the 1940s, the museum received unique exhibits from the former Museum of New Western Art (the collections of S. Shchukin and I. Morozov). These two major Moscow collectors who had created their own private museums at the turn of the century were blessed with true foresight as a result of their passion for art, thorough knowledge and impeccable artistic taste. They discovered Impressionism unrecognized even in Paris yet.

Museum exhibit. Italian courtyard

Giovanni Antonio Boltraffio.
Saint Sebastian

◀ Lucas Cranach.
Madonna and the Child

Paul Gauguin. The Queen
(The King's Wife). 1896

Pierre-Auguste Renoir.
Girls in Black. Early 1880s

The collection compiled by
S. Shchukin was considered the
best in Europe. Both collections
were displayed in the owner's
residence and open to the public.
Several young artists who came
to view the exhibits later became
world-famous representatives
of the Russian avant garde.

After receiving these private
collections the Museum of Fine
Arts gained considerable status
among the major world museums. At present its holdings
number more than a million original paintings and graphic works,
and even more sculptures and
objects of applied art from all
over the world, from antiquity
to the present day. In 1985 the
Museum of Private Collections
was established as a department
of the main museum.

Church of St John the Soldier at Yakimanka. 1709–13

TVERSKAYA STREET

Tverskaya (in the Soviet period Gorky) Street is the main street of Moscow. Known since the 14th century it became the city's major thoroughfare in the 15th – 17th centuries when relations with north-western Russian principalities, primarily Tver and Novgorod, began to play an important part in Moscow's economy. Another impact was given to its development in the 18th century when the new capital of St Petersburg was founded in the north. It was Tverskaya Street that all who came to Moscow from St Petersburg and vice versa travelled along.

Building of the Main Telegraph Office in Tverskaya Street

Office of the Moscow City Council in Tverskaya Street

*Monument to Prince Yury Dolgoruky. 1954. Sculptors
S. Orlov, A. Antropov and N. Shtamm, architect V. Andreyev*

Though the street might be greatly changed, it retained its representative character. It was wider and busier and looked more ceremonial than other streets. In accordance with the Soviet plan for Moscow's reconstruction Gorky Street was the first to undergo certain improvements. Some of its buildings were demolished, others moved to other sites as a result of which the street became 2.5 times wider, thus the architects emphasized its leading role among other streets.

Tverskaya Street links several squares. Pushkin (former Strastnaya) Square, though much altered, better than others answers its original purpose of public square. The history of another square is no less complicated. It came into existence in the late 18th century when it was designed by M. Kazakov as a drill ground in front of the Moscow Governor-General house. In the second half of the 1930s it was widened and built with multi-storeyed houses, thus assuming more austere and ceremonial character to match the style of the Moscow City Council Office (where the city authorities sit now) that stands in it.

Tverskaya Street

*Pushkin Square. Monument to Alexander Pushkin. 1880.
Sculptor A. Opekushin*

CATHEDRALS AND CHURCHES

Cathedral of Christ the Saviour. Interior

The Cathedral of Christ the Saviour is situated in the city centre, not far from the Kremlin, on the high bank of the Moscow River (Kropotkinskaya Embankment). Built in commemoration of a great event in Russian history — the glorious victory over Napoleon's army in 1812, the structure was to be in accord with the architectural composition of the nearby Kremlin, Moscow's historical centre, and was modelled on the Kremlin cathedrals of the Dormition and the Archangel Michael.

Its size is enormous: it is 103 m high, its area 6 805 m^2, the central dome's diameter 25.5 m. Construction of this grandiose edifice which could accommodate 10 000 people went on for dozens of years. The foundation was laid in 1839, the construction work completed in the 1880s and the consecration of the cathedral took place in 1889 after which daily services began there.

◀ *Cathedral of Christ the Saviour. Designed by K. Thon. Reconstructed in the 1990s*

Chapel in front of the Cathedral of Christ the Saviour

materials have been applied. In the January of 2000 it was consecrated and opened for daily services.

Numerous fires devastated Moscow in the past when most of its buildings were wooden. The 14th-century chronicle mentions "six great fires" which burnt the city to ashes. Moscow was also greatly damaged by foreign invaders. That's why very few samples of ancient architecture are preserved now. But the less they are in number, the more we value them as unique creations of Russian genius. Most of the churches were stone so they could withstand both fires and invaders.

In one of the oldest parts of Moscow, Khamovniki, a few ancient buildings including the Church of St Nicholas have survived. In the 17th century there used to be water meadows owned by the grand prince. Soon *khamovniki*, court weavers, were settled here, hence the name of the district. They built the Church of St Nicholas and decorated it with three tiers of *kokoshniks* (semicircular false gables) and bright multi-coloured tiles. Its elegant bell tower topped with a hipped roof is of special note. It has a lacelike pattern due to the numerous openings which make the acoustics better.

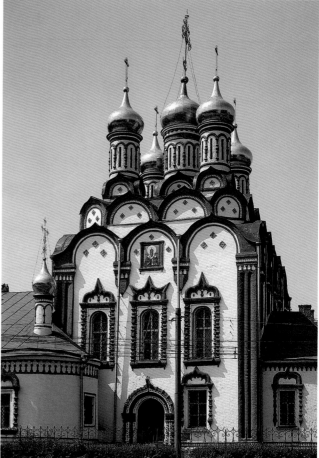

The cathedral was lavishly decorated. A marble band with basreliefs showing Biblical scenes ran along the facades, above the portals. The murals inside were painted by the famous Russian artists V. Surikov, V. Vereshchagin, K. Makovsky, G. Semiradsky and others.

In 1931 the cathedral was exploded, later a swimming pool opened on the site. In the 1990s donations were made by thousands of people from all over the country and the cathedral was completely reconstructed on the original site. It looks exactly like the original structure, though the latest methods and

Church of St George on Pskov Hill. 1657

Church of St Nicholas at Khamovniki. 1679–82

Church of the Holy Trinity at Bersenevo (with the side altar of St Nicholas). 1654

Church of the Intercession at Fili. Iconostasis

The Church of the Intercession at Fili has been a branch of the Andrey Rublev Central Museum of Ancient Russian Culture and Art since 1972.

Built by an unknown architect on the ancestorial estate of the boyar Lev Naryshkin, uncle of Peter the Great, the church is a striking example of the Moscow Baroque style. Stylistic solemnity and picturesque ornamentation of both the interior and exterior of the church are equally impressive. The lofty, bright interior features a proliferation of gilded woodcarving, the multi-tiered iconostasis, the tsar's balcony suspended above the arch at the entrance, the icon cases and framed entrance archways. Rich decoration of the interior creates an impression of radiance, festivity and lavish splendour. Karp Zolotaryov, one of the leading masters of the royal Armoury and head of the Ambassadorial Workshop, provided the inspiration and expertise for the iconostasis, woodcarving and gilding.

The boyars' residences were located not far from the church surrounded by a park with ponds and the first regular plantations to appear in Moscow.

Church of the Intercession at Fili. 1693

Cathedral of the Theophany at Yelokhovo. 1837–45. Architect Yu. Tiurin

OLD MOSCOW

Extant in present-day Moscow are a number of dwelling houses built after the fire of 1812. These include not only some unique architectural structures but also standardized buildings made from specially designed models. When we look at them we can imagine a quiet and old-fashioned life lived by the owners of these houses that once were scattered all over Moscow. Moscow's mansions have an air of cosiness, and we can't but remember the words of outstanding Russian literary critic Vissarion Belinsky: "For a Russian who was born in St Petersburg Moscow is as striking and inspiring as for a foreigner". Osip Bove, Domenico Gilliardi and Afanasy Grigoryev were among the best-known architects of the period dwelling houses and mansions. In contrast to St Petersburg Moscow has very few Baroque structures. One of them is the former mansion of M. Apraksin, later owned by the Trubetskoys. It is a fine and rare example of the late Baroque

Memorial house of Fyodor Chaliapin. 18th-century mansion

In one of the "quiet" corners in Moscow

style. Lavishly decorated it looks like a palace from the period so in the past it used to be attributed to Rastrelli. Later, in the epoch of Classicism, it was ironically called a "chest of drawers".

At the end of the 19th century many-storeyed apartment houses for rent appeared in Moscow. One of these is the house of Z. Pertsova — imitation of old Russian wooden architecture. This typical Art Nouveau edifice is one of the most impressive and festive-looking in Moscow. Especially noteworthy are the complex configuration of the house, its steeply-pitched roof, ceramic representations of the sun, mermaids, exotic animals and plants. The ornamentation of its facades combines polychrome majolica and sculpture designed by S. Maliutin who has contributed a lot to the development of Russian applied art.

Among the most interesting historical and architectural monuments of the great artistic value on Nikolskaya Street is the Royal Print Yard, which played a great role in the advance of learning in this country. Here Ivan Fyodorov and Piotr Mstislavets printed the first dated Russian book in 1564. The territory that it occupied is now concealed behind the unusual building of the former Synod printing house. Its main facade is in the Russian Gothic manner, although the compositional structure is typical of Classicism. Today the building is occupied by the University of Humanities.

Pertsova's apartment house. 1906–10. Architect N. Zhukov, artist S. Maliutin

Mansion. 19th century

Mansion of M. Apraksin — the Trubetskoys. 1760

Building of the former Loan Bank. 1913–16. Architects V. Pokrovsky and B. Nilus

Nikolskaya Street. Building of the former Synod printing house. 1814. Architect I. Mironovsky ▶

Extant at present are woodcarving on the front door, the handrails of the staircase, the doors of the flats and even the coat stand in the entrance hall. The owners' rooms all covered with woodcarving and painting were extremely beautiful.

The building of the Loan Bank is designed in the Neo-Russian style. Its central facade combining the representative character of modern public institution with the elegance of 17th-century palace is most impressive.

Mansion of Riabushinsky. 1900. Architect F. Shekhtel

MANSION OF RIABUSHINSKY

Moscow's buildings designed in the Art Nouveau style that came into fashion in the early 20th century, are of great interest. The style was brought about by the quest for new forms in architecture. New types of construction, building materials and functional decisions were introduced then. The architects kept their interest in the historical prototypes of the 19th-century architecture but applied them to another artistic system oriented towards painting and based on the contrast of rationalism and free use of various styles in decoration.

Most famous Art Nouveau structures in Moscow are those designed by F. Shekhtel, the Riabushinsky mansion being one of them. Stepan Riabushinsky was one of the members of the family of wealthy Russian industrialists. Descended from peasants, they successfully invested in textiles, land, and banking in the 19th and early 20th centuries. The owner of the mansion was known mainly as a collector of French art.

Apartments in the Riabushinsky mansion (Maksim Gorky's museum) are arranged in accordance with the Art Nouveau principle – from the inside to the outside, from the centre to the adjacent volumes. All the rooms are grouped round the main staircase gradually winding upwards, which has elegant curved rails. The exterior outline is simple and clear-cut. It is made of contrasting geometrical forms, its decor is irregular, yet natural.

Mansion of Riabushinsky. Main staircase

PETER CASTLE

The structure was intended to be a palace, but as it has the form of a castle it is better known as the Peter (Petrovsky) Castle. Its fortified wall with several tiers of tall faceted towers, smaller round towers and battlements makes it look like a fantastic mediaeval fortress. The main building of the palace is even more striking. Its ground floor with the lancet-shaped windows is decorated with low pitcher-shaped pillars. The attic has a sophisticated roof with numerous big and small pediments in the style reminiscent of Baroque. The palace is crowned with a dome placed upon a high drum which has many windows with rich ornamentation. The dome looks like one of those huge splendid cups that once graced the feasts of Russian tsars.

With this structure M. Kazakov set the so-called new Russian (Neo-Russian) trend, characteristic of Moscow architecture, in the Art Nouveau style. Many projects for the Kremlin development were designed in the style. The top of the Nikolskaya Tower and the Synod printing house in Nikolskaya Street as well as some others imitate Gothic structures.

Peter Castle (Peter Palace).
1776–96. Architect M. Kazakov

NOVODEVICHY CONVENT

The Novodevichy Convent, one of the most beautiful monastic ensembles in Russia, has been a branch of the State Historical Museum since 1934. It was founded by order of Prince Vasily III in 1524, to commemorate the 1514 victory of Russia over the Polish and Lithuanian forces in the battle for the borderlands and the return of the town of Smolensk. Situated near the road leading to Moscow from the south, it served as a military outpost on more than one occasion. The convent was favoured by the tsars and boyars, since the nuns included members of both royal and high-ranking families. The architectural ensemble was formed from the 16th to 17th centuries. The ancient convent cathedral was dedicated to the Smolensk icon of the Mother of God coming from Byzantium. It was a mostly revered icon in the Smolensk Province.

*Panoramic view of the Novodevichy
Convent from the pond*

*Cathedral of the Smolensk Icon
of the Mother of God. 1524–25;
bell tower. 1689–90*

*Cathedral of the Smolensk Icon
of the Mother of God. Iconostasis*

Panoramic view of the St Andronicus Monastery of the Saviour from the bank of the River Yauza

*Icon of St George with episodes
from his life and miracles in
the borderscenes. Early 16th century*

ST ANDRONICUS MONASTERY OF THE SAVIOUR

The white walls of one of the oldest Moscow monasteries stand on the high bank of the Yauza, the second largest river in Moscow, at the mouth of the Zolotoy Rozhok tributary. The St Andronicus Monastery of the Saviour was founded in the mid-14th century by Metropolitan Alexius, to commemorate his miraculous deliverence from death in a storm that occured during his homeward voyage from Constantinople. In olden times the monastery served as an important outpost. The architectural ensemble was built over several centuries: the Cathedral of the Saviour from the late 14th to early 15th century, the monastery refectory from 1504 to 1506, the refectory Church of the Archangel Michael from 1691 to 1729, the walls and towers from the 17th to 18th centuries, and the monastic cells and guesthouse from the 18th to 19th century. The monastery is most famous as the place where the great monk and icon-painter Andrey Rublev led his ascetic life. Rublev died here and was buried beside the Cathedral of the Saviour in about 1430.

Cathedral of the Saviour. 1410–27

◀ *Panoramic view of Zamoskvorechye*

State Tretyakov Gallery. 1902–04. Designed by V. Vasnetsov

Icon of the Old Testament Trinity. By Andrey Rublev. 1410s

STATE TRETYAKOV GALLERY

The Tretyakov Gallery is one of the most famous art museums in the world. Its collection covers a whole millennium of Russian cultural development.

The founder was a Moscow merchant and industrialist who was also a great art expert, connoisseur and renowned patron: Pavel Tretyakov. He devoted his entire life to forming a collection. Every year he added what he considered to be the finest works of art to the gallery, buying paintings directly from the artists or from exhibitions.

The already-famous gallery was opened to public view in 1881, during Tretyakov's lifetime. In 1892, just a few years before his death, Tretyakov donated his superb collection to the city of Moscow.

The famous colourful facade uniting the entire complex of buildings was erected after the death of Tretiakov between 1901 and 1903, to a design by eminent Russian artist V. Vasnetsov. This Russian-style structure is a symbol of national art.

Today the collection consists of more than 100 000 works of art displayed at the department of ancient Russian art from the 12th to 17th centuries, the department of graphics and sculpture from the 18th to early 20th centuries and the department of 20th-century art.

Ivan Shishkin. Morning in a Pine Forest. *1889*

Victor Vasnetsov. Warriors. *1898*

Valentin Surikov. Boyarynya Morozova. *1887*

◀ *Karl Briullov*. Rider. *1832*

Vasily Perov. Hunters Resting. *1871*

MOSCOW HIGH-RISE BUILDINGS

From the second half of the 1930s to 1950s a great number of buildings that can boast perfect artistic quality were constructed in Moscow. The architectural trend once labelled as "excessive embellishment" is no longer condemned. It is considered to be the Neo-Classical style now. At that time the architects were eager to create ensembles that would be in harmony with their elevated, triumphant mood and represent the ideals of the epoch. They were deliberate in using sumptuous, imposing forms. Such ensembles appeared in Tverskaya (former Gorky) Street and part of Kutuzovsky Prospect reconstructed before the 1950s.

Udarnik *cinema. 1921–31. Architects B. and D. Iofann*

Dwelling house for the Central Executive Committee staff on Bersenyevskaya Embankment (known as the "House on the embankment"). 1928–31. Architects B. and D. Iofann

Administration office and dwelling house. 1949–53. Architects A. Dushkin
and B. Mezentsev

Most important architectural complexes to be created all over Moscow at the period were the standardized high-rise buildings erected in commemoration of the 800th anniversary of Moscow and metro stations. The buildings of Moscow University, different ministries on Smolenskaya and Komsomolskaya Squares as well as dwelling houses on Kotelnicheskaya Embankment and Vosstaniya Square added some new features to Moscow's outline, creating new vertical lines round which many districts' compositions were grouped and which were perceived as the components of the one grandiose plan.

◀ Office of the Ministry of Foreign
Affairs in Smolenskaya Square.
1948–53. Architects V. Gelfreich
and M. Minkus

Main building of Moscow University
on Vorobyovy Hills. 1949–53.
Architects L. Rudnev, P. Abrosimov
and A. Khryakov

Central Sports Complex at Luzhniki.
1955–56, 1979–80. Architects
A. Vlasov, I. Rozhin and N. Ullas

Crimean Bridge. 1938. Engineer
B. Konstantinov, architect A. Vlasov.
One of the biggest chain bridges
in Europe

VDNKh

The present-day Exhibition Complex has been created on the basis of the former Exhibition of National Economic Achievements (VDNKh) opened in 1959. Its pavilions are typical examples of the Soviet architecture from the 1930s to 1950s. Eminent architects of the period V. Shchuko, V. Gelfreich and others participated in the project. The *Friendship of the Peoples* and *Stone Flower* fountains are located in the central alley.

The well-known monument by V. Mukhina, once expressing the Soviet ideal, the *Worker and Collective-farm Woman*, stands at the main entrance. It embellished the Soviet pavilion at the International Exhibition in Paris in 1937.

Main entrance to the Exhibition Complex (the former Exhibition of National Economic Achievements)

Central alley with the Stone Flower *fountain*

Friendship of the Peoples *fountain. 1953.*
Architect K. Topuridze, sculptor D. Konstantinovsky

Main pavilion of the Exhibition Complex. 1954.
Architect V. Shchuko ▶

Office of the Russian Federation government on Krasnopresnenskaya Embankment. 1981.
Architect D. Chechulin

NEW ARBAT. THE WHITE HOUSE

The section of Kalinin Prospect between Arbat Square and Sadovoye (Garden) Ring is another sight of present-day Moscow. The project worked out by a team of architects was awarded the Grand Prix by the Paris Centre of Architectural Research in 1966 for the renewal of architectural forms and achievements in working out long-term construction projects. The super modern style of this thoroughfare is made up by the geometrical regularity of its lines and the obvious repetitions and sharp contrasts of the forms. The verticals of the twenty-six-storey tower-shaped blocks rhythmically alternate with the lower, somewhat flattened, rectangular buildings that house cafes, bars, restaurants (including the *Tropicana* and *Metelitsa*) and shops (including the *Novoarbatsky*, a largest supermarket in the capital).

The light-coloured twenty-storey building that rises above Krasnopresnenskaya Embankment is known as the White House, as it is the seat of Russia's government. Its design is rather peculiar. The building consists of two parts. Above the lower seven-storey part with the side-wings there rises the narrower and taller part crowned by a small tower with a clock and the Russian Federation flag. A broad staircase leads up to the entrance, in front of which there is a wide square. Before designing the edifice the author headed a group of architects who created the *Russia* hotel, the largest in Moscow.

Arbat Square. The Prague *restaurant. Reconstructed in 1955. Architect B. Sobolevsky*

New Arbat (Kalinin Prospect). 1963–68. Architects M. Posokhin, A. Mndoyantz, G. Makarevich, B. Tkhor, Sh. Ayrapetov, I. Pokrovsky, Yu. Popov and A. Zaytsev

VICTORY MEMORIAL

The Victory Memorial was opened in commemoration of the 50th anniversary of the victory in World War II (known in Russia as the Great Patriotic War). The memorial complex includes a museum (its displays are dedicated to the events of 1941–45), Conquerors' Square adorned with the allegorical figure of the goddess of Victory, "Years of War" alley and the Orthodox Church of St George decorated with huge bronze basreliefs. There is also a synagogue and a mosque.

◀ *Moscow at night. Multi-storeyed dwelling house on Kotelnicheskaya Embankment*

Victory Memorial dedicated to the victory in the Great Patriotic War of 1941–45 on Poklonnaya Hill. 1983–95. Architects A. Poliansky, V. Budayev, L. Vavakin, sculptor Z Tsereteli

Raushskaya Embankment with the Balchug *hotel (on the left)*

Cosmos *hotel. 1976–79. Architects T. Zaikin, V. Steiskaya, O. Cacoub, P. Jougleaux and S. Epstein*

HOTELS

Moscow is a major tourist and business centre. Many comfortable hotels coming up to the highest standards have recently been erected here.

The *Cosmos* (*Space*) hotel which can accommodate 3 600 people ranks among the hotels of the first international class. Located opposite the *VDNKh* metro station, in Mira (Peace) Prospect, the building was designed by Russian and French architects

Renaissance *and* Ukraina *hotels, most fashionable in Moscow* and engineers and constructed by a French firm. The upper part of this very tall structure comprising twenty-seven storeys has the shape of a cemi-cylinder, or an arc. It forms a sort of mighty axis oriented towards the complex of the former Exhibition of Economic Achievements. Its facades are very impressive: their smoky goldish colour is created by the combination of the anodized aluminium of the walls and the dark-coloured glass of the windows. The buliding demonstrates a high quality of both construction and decoration work. The hotel has a well-equipped conference hall, a transformable banqueting hall, restaurants, cafes, bars, buffets, a swimming pool with a "beach" terrace, saunas and a bowling alley.

After the reconstruction the *Balchug* hotel has turned into a hotel of high European standard. The range of services provided and comfortableness put it among the most famous hotels of the world. The *Renaissance* (former *Olimpic*) and *President* (former *Oktyabrskaya*) are also de luxe hotels.

METRO

Moscow's metro stations called the "underground palaces" of Moscow are another attraction of the city. It is not an exaggeration as their interiors demonstrate almost royal splendour. Used in their decoration are more than twenty varieties of marble coming from the Urals, Altai, Central Asia, the Caucases and Ukraine as well as labradorite, granite, porphyry, rhodonite, onyx and other natural stones. The magnificent, festive-looking halls and vestibules are adorned with sculpture, basreliefs, mosaics, paintings, stained glass panels and murals executed by the best artists.

The Moscow underground was designed and built by eminent Soviet architects who aimed not only at utility and comfort but gave every station a unique look. The metro station *Mayakovskaya* opened in 1938 is considered one of the most beautiful. Its underground vestibule is supported by metal columns faced with granite and stainless steel. Mosaics in the cupolas were made after the sketches of A. Deineka. In 1937 the *Mayakovskaya* station was awarded the Grand Prix at the International Exhibition in Paris as the first deep underground station supported with columns. At the same exhibition Moscow's metro stations of the first line were given a prize for perfect urban design.

The metro stations *Mayakovskaya*, *Kropotkinskaya*, *Ploshchad Sverdlova*, *Prospect Mira* and *Kurskaya-Radialnaya* are fine examples of the architecture from the 1930s to 1950s. Some of them are protected by the state as national property.

Underground vestibule of the metro station Kiyevskaya-Koltsevaya *(in the circular line). 1954. Architects Ye. Katonin, V. Skugarev and G. Golubev*

Underground vestibule of the metro station Mayakovskaya. *1938. Architect A. Dushkin*

Underground vestibule of the metro station Komsomolskaya-Koltsevaya *(in the circular line). 1952. Architects A. Shchusev, V. Kakorin and A. Zabolotskaya*

The first metro line began to operate in Moscow on May 15, 1935.

New stations built nowadays are of simple and austere design. The passengers are guided by the metro plans which are to be found in every upper entrance hall, indicators and recorded information.

Underground vestibule of the metro station Arbatskaya. *1953. Architects L. Poliakov and V. Pilevin*

Underground vestibule of the metro station Taganskaya–Koltsevaya *(in the circular line)*.
1950. Architects K. Ryzhov and A. Medvedev

*Underground vestibule
of the metro station* Ploshchad Revoliutsii. *1938. Architect A. Dushkin*

Northern River Port at Khimki. 1937. Architects A. Rukhlyadev and V. Krinsky, sculptor I. Yefimov

ARRIVING BY AIR, BY RIVER AND RAIL

The Northern River Port is noteworthy for its architecture. It looks like a huge steamer. An open gallery supported by 150 four-edged columns of white stone runs along the perimeter on its ground floor. The tower with its high spire is like a navigating bridge. A wide staircase descends from the central portal to the landing stage. Comfortable liners start from here on long voyages to Astrakhan, Rostov-on-Don and St Petersburg.

The Leningrad Railway Station is a replica of the Moscow Station built in St Petersburg. The building is organically integrated into the ensemble of Komsomolskaya Square. Trains leave this station for St Petersburg, Petrozavodsk and Murmansk. Comfortable express trains (*Krasnaya Strela*, *Aurora*, *Russkaya Troika* and others) run between Moscow and St Petersburg.

Leningrad (former Nicholas) Railway Station in Komsomolskaya Square. 1849. Architect K. Thon

Airport Sheremetyevo II. 1979. Architects G. Yelkin, G. Kriukov and M. Chesakova, engineers N. Irmes, V. Aksenov and A. Pritzker

The Sheremetyevo Airport, Moscow's air gate, has been operating as international airport since 1965. The Sheremetyevo II eight-storey building made of aluminium and dark-coloured glass is equipped with the latest, most modern devices which can provide safe landing for all types of aircrafts.

KOLOMENSKOYE

The State Historical, Architectural and Landscape Museum of Kolomenskoye is located in the south of Moscow. Kolomenskoye was particularly important during the reign of Ivan the Terrible in the 16th century and Alexey Mikhailovich in the 17th century. The unique architectural ensemble was built at this period. The dominant structure at Kolomenskoye is the Church of the Ascension. In the 16th century it served as a summer church for the tsar's family. It was erected to mark a momentous event – the birth of a long-awaited heir to the Russian throne, the future Ivan IV, called Ivan the Terrible. The church reaches a height of 62 m.

Kolomenskoye.
Church of the Ascension. 1532

Kolomenskoye. Church of the Kazan
Icon of the Mother of God. 1649–50

Festival of folk music in Kolomenskoye

KUSKOVO

Kuskovo is first mentioned as the country estate of the boyar V. Sheremetyev at the beginning of the 16th century. In 1918 private land was nationalized and the last owner relinquished the estate to the Soviet government. The entire territory of Kuskovo became part of the south-eastern region of Moscow in 1960. The famous palace ensemble and park appeared in the second half of the 18th century. Count Pyotr

Sheremetyev, an important member of the nobility at the Russian Imperial Court, state functionary and collector of art and antiquities was its first owner. Count Sheremetyev had the mansion built not just as a recreational summer residence, but as a focus for different art forms appreciated by experts and connoisseurs. A large part of his vast collection of fine and applied art was displayed here.

Kuskovo is the oldest park on the outskirts of Moscow, although what remains is only part of the sweeping expanse that was once the pride of the Sheremetyevs. The regular French-style park was laid out in the 1750s – 1760s and featured pavilions, a conservatory and a collection of marble sculpture.

Kuskovo was visited by Catherine the Great on several occasions. Up to 25 000 guests would flock here to lavish celebrations. The count decreed that the park should be open to the public in the summer months.

In 1932 the Porcelain Museum was transferred here. Today it has a unique collection of ceramics produced by Russian and foreign factories from the 15th to 20th centuries and numbering 18 000 items.

Kuskovo. French-style regular park

◀ *Kuskovo. Palace. Second vestibule*

Ostankino. Palace. 1792–98. Architects F. Camporesi, A. Mironov, P. Argunov and others

OSTANKINO

The Ostankino Theatre-Palace became famous worldwide two centuries ago. The idea of creating a temple to the arts was realized at Ostankino by its owner Nikolay Sheremetyev. The theatre had special machinery which produced special effects and the stage and auditorium could be transformed into a ballroom. A troupe of trained serf actors performed the best operas by both Western European and Russian composers. There were some 100 operas in their repertoire.
The lovely Praskovya Kovalyova-Zhemchugova, darling of the public, performed with the company and became the wife of Count Sheremetyev in defiance of social convention.

The Ostankino palace was filled with family collections of paintings, sculpture, antique firearms and porcelain. The picture gallery once exhibited paintings by Titian, Rubens and Van Dyck but it was looted by Napoleon's soldiers in 1812. Ostankino park employed both the English and French systems of landscape gardening, and was renowned for a rare collection of exotic foreign plants.

Palace. Theatre. Auditorium   *Palace. Western part of the ground floor*

TSARITSYNO

Tsaritsyno is a historical museum of art and architecture in a landscaped park. The picturesque palace ensemble and park at Tsaritsyno, in the south-eastern outskirts of Moscow, date from the second half of the 18th century. In 1775 Catherine the Great decided to build a residence here, from that time onwards the area was called Tsaritsyno.

Design and construction of the ensemble was entrusted to the eminent Russian architect Vasily Bazhenov. The idea of creating an estate in the Romantic style was realized in an architectural ensemble that obeyed the strict laws of Classicism. By using the forms of ancient

Tsaritsyno. Grand Bridge over the ravine, view from the pond. 1776–85.
Architect V. Bazhenov

Servants' house. 1776–85. Architect V. Bazhenov

Russian architecture, stylizing them and adapting them to a new environment, Bazhenov created a novel architectural and environmental ensemble.

Contemporaries enthused at the work of the great Bazhenov. But fate struck and condemned the estate for the next two centuries. Catherine the Great was displeased with the palace and ordered it to be completely demolished. Modern historians believe Catherine was angered by Bazhenov's intimacy with "freethinkers" and the Masonic followers of Paul, heir to the throne.

In 1927 a museum was opened in the estate.

Tsaritsyno. Grand Palace

Tsaritsyno. Fancy-shaped bridge over the road to Moscow. 1776–85. Architect V. Bazhenov

Trinity–St Sergius Monastery

The famous Trinity–St Sergius Monastery where ascetic life has not ceased up to now is situated not far from Moscow on the road to Yaroslavl. It was founded in 1354 by St Sergius who had come to live in the then deserted and desolate place from the nearby town of Radonezh. St Sergius was greatly revered by Russian people for his spiritual gifts and when Prince Dmitry Donskoy went to fight with the Tartars, he came to ask for his blessing.

The monastery's magnificent ensemble was built over six centuries. The Cathedral of the Holy Trinity was erected to commemorate St Sergius' immense service to the state. Here at St Sergius' shrine Moscow princes kissed the cross swearing to keep their promises and treaties and prayed before going to wars and on coming back from them.

◄ *Panoramic view of the Trinity–St Sergius Monastery from the south-east*

Piatnitskaya Tower. 1640

Krasnogorsky chapel. 1760

Inside the Trinity Cathedral was painted by the famous icon-painters Andrey Rublev and Daniil Chorny. Unfortunately, in 1635 their frescoes were replaced with new ones which were also repainted not once. The 16th-century silver shrine of St Sergius graces the cathedral. The canopy was set up over it in 1737. It is one of the main places of pilgrimage for Orthodox Christians.

Opposite the Trinity Cathedral there stands the Church of the Holy Spirit, or the Church of the Descent of the Holy Spirit on the Apostles, built in 1476 by Pskov masters.

The most important building in the ensemble is the Cathedral of the Dormition (1559–85) modelled on the Kremlin cathedral of the same name. A small stone structure with the hipped roof by its north-west corner houses the tomb of Boris Godunov and his family.

The most festive-looking building is the Refectory Church with its side-altar dedicated to St Sergius (1686–92).

Cathedral of the Dormition.
1559–85. Chapel on the well. Late 17th century

Noteworthy among the 17th-century structures is a very tall five-tier bell tower. Begun in 1740 by Ivan Michurin and completed only in the 1770s after the design of D. Ukhtomsky, it became the dominant stucture of the ensemble.

The monastery is enclosed with the fortified wall featured by eleven towers which were built in the 16th century. In the 17th century their height was increased twice. The wall consists of three defence tiers. The lower one contains deeply set casemates and embrasures, the middle tier is a vaulted gallery with loop-holes and the upper one is a gallery with battlements.

Bell tower. 1740–70.
Architects I. Michurin and
D. Ukhtomsky

Cathedral of the Holy Trinity. 1422

Church of the Holy Ghost. 1476

Cathedral of the Holy Trinity.
Iconostasis and St Sergius' shrine ▶

Feast day in the Trinity–St Sergius Monastery

Gateway Church of St John the Baptist. 1699

Moscow

P-2 Art Publishers, St Petersburg
Amarant Publishers, Moscow

PRINTED AND BOUND BY THE IVAN FIODOROV PRINTING COMPANY, ST PETERSBURG (1548)